D0515778

Dancing Elephants
and
Floating Continents

THE STORY OF CANADA BENEATH YOUR FEET

JOHN WILSON

KEY PORTER BOOKS

For Sarah—JW

A special thank you to Dr. Ron Clowes, Director of Lithoprobe, who provided advice on the scientific content of the book and assisted with the preparation of several illustrations.

National Library of Canada Cataloguing in Publication Data

Wilson, John (John Alexander), 1951–

    Dancing elephants and floating continents : the story of Canada beneath your feet / John Wilson.

Includes index.

ISBN 1-55263-200-8

1. Geodynamics—Juvenile literature. 2. Geomorphology —Juvenile literature. I. Title.

QE501.25.W54 2003   j550   C2003-900523-2

The Canada Council | Le Conseil des Arts
for the Arts | du Canada

ONTARIO ARTS COUNCIL
CONSEIL DES ARTS DE L'ONTARIO

The publisher gratefully acknowledges the support of the Canada Council for the Arts and the Ontario Arts Council for its publishing program.

We acknowledge the financial support of the Government of Canada through the Book Publishing Industry Development Program (BPIDP) for our publishing activities.

The author and publisher also acknowledge the financial support for this book from Lithoprobe: a national geo-science research project funded by the Natural Sciences and Engineering Research Council (NSERC) of Canada and the Geological Survey of Canada.

Key Porter Books Limited
70 The Esplanade
Toronto, Ontario
Canada M5E 1R2

www.keyporter.com

Photo credits: Canadian Press Archives: pages 13, 15, 23, 32, 33, 41; Natural Resources Canada (Geological Survey of Canada): page 13 (bottom), 43; Lithoprobe: pages: 5, 37; Todd Korol: pages 6-7 (top); U.S. Geological Survey: pages 26, 27, 39; Jerry Greer Photography: page 28

Illustration credits: All illustrations created by Visutronx Services, except: pages 14 and 30 by Vesna Krstanovich; page 38, by Alan Barnard

Design: Jack Steiner

Printed and bound in China

03 04 05 06 07 5 4 3 2 1

Contents

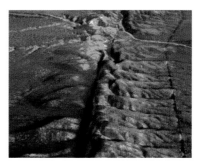

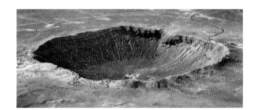

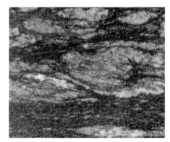

Dancing on the World

How do you tell the difference between an African elephant and an Indian elephant? Think about your last trip to the zoo, or that television show you once watched. Having trouble? Okay. The African elephant is bigger, has larger ears and is more aggressive.

Now for the really tough question. How do you tell the difference between an African or Indian elephant and a Canadian elephant?

Canadian elephant? Wait a minute, you're probably saying, outside of zoos there aren't any elephants in Canada. Well, you're right and you're wrong. For some time now, a herd of Canadian elephants has been spotted in various places from Vancouver to Halifax and from the shores of Lake Superior to the Yukon Territory.

Okay, so they're not real elephants. Canadian elephants are actually 25-ton trucks (that's as much as four African elephants!) that have been nicknamed Dancing Elephants because they pound the ground with huge hammers and make it shake just the way a herd of real elephants does.

Why? Good question.

Have you ever dropped a pebble into a smooth pond? When the pebble breaks the surface of the water, it creates waves that spread out in all directions. When these waves hit the edge of the pond, or a rock sticking up through the water, their outward-spreading motion is stopped, and the waves change direction, heading back toward the pebble.

The hammers that pound the ground underneath Dancing Elephants create waves that work in a similar way, but with two big differences. First, these waves—called shock waves—are so powerful that they can travel for tens of kilometers through the Earth's crust, bounce off of something and travel all the way back to the surface. Scientists find this extremely helpful. By measuring the amount of time it takes for the shock waves to bounce back, they can determine just how far below the Earth's surface an object is.

The second big difference between shock waves and pond waves is that shock waves can't be seen—but they can be heard. When Dancing Elephants pound the ground, microphones are placed nearby to pick up the sound of the shock waves that are being reflected back. These micro-

Dancing Elephant trucks pound the ground, sending out shock waves that bounce off the layers of rock and are picked up by microphones.

AN ELEPHANT'S WORK

Dancing Elephants have been used for many years by exploration companies in search of oil, gas and minerals. However, Lithoprobe scientists, and others, adapted the procedure to look deep into the Earth's crust.

For this purpose, the Elephants' operators must synchronize the pounding action of the hammers. If this is not done properly, the vibrations from one truck will wipe out the record from the others, and not even Lithoprobe's sophisticated computers or the specialists who interpret the results will be able to sort out the mess. Usually four or five trucks are sufficient, but on one occasion in southern Alberta Lithoprobe used 12—a feat never before achieved, and one that enabled scientists to look 100 kilometers into the Earth.

phones are connected to computers that turn the sounds into a picture.

Over the past 20 years, the Dancing Elephants have produced hundreds of pictures. These images, and the Elephants themselves, are part of Lithoprobe—a project that is trying to discover how Canada formed over the last 4 billion years. The pictures are of things that no human will ever see. They are snapshots of a world far beneath our feet; pictures of

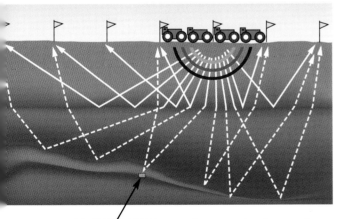

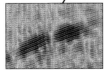

To the untrained eye, they look like wavy lines, but a geophysicist can read the story they tell.

what the world was like long ago. They give scientists a lot of information about geology and about where to look for minerals, but they do something else as well: they tell a story.

And what a story! The characters are entire continents—moving around the surface of the Earth, crashing into each other, crushing islands, raising mountain ranges, and opening and closing vast oceans—and the plot is nothing less than the formation of the planet on which we live.

Mapping What Can't Be Seen

Five hundred years ago, a man sat in the wave-tossed cabin of his small ship and dipped a quill pen in ink. His name was John Cabot, and the few kilometers of the Newfoundland coast that he roughly marked on his chart that day were the beginning of a vast undertaking that is still continuing—the mapping of Canada.

In 1497, no one knew what Canada looked like. Gradually, though, a picture began to emerge as others added to Cabot's work. Champlain mapped the St. Lawrence River, Hudson discovered his bay, Vancouver sailed around his island, Franklin struggled along the Arctic Coast, and countless other adventurers suffered and died to add to the picture.

Today, satellites can photograph Canada from space, and cars, trains and planes can take you almost anywhere you want to go. Thanks to all of this, we know what Canada looks like: broad at the bottom where it joins the United States, and narrowing to a bewildering collection of icy islands that reach almost to the North Pole. We know about the Great Lakes, the Prairies and the Rocky Mountains. The map of Canada appears to be complete.

Not quite!

Only part of Canada is mapped; only two of four dimensions. Yes, we know what the breadth and width of Canada looks like. We have mapped from Vancouver to Halifax and from Windsor to Ellesmere Island—but what about the depth? Caves, mines and drill holes (for oil and minerals) only go a short way down. Canada's depths are a true mystery, and so is its fourth dimension: time.

Let's say that 2 billion years ago you were able to look down on Canada from space. You wouldn't recognize a thing. There were no Great Lakes, no Prairies and no Rocky Mountains—only some very

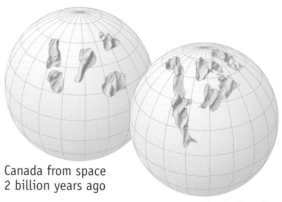

Canada from space
2 billion years ago

North America
70 million years ago

The continents never look the same for long. The moving plates of the Earth's crust are continually crashing into one another, causing earthquakes and volcanic eruptions and creating mountain chains.

LITHO-WHAT?

The word Lithoprobe comes from the Greek *lithos*, meaning "rock," and the Latin *probare*, meaning "to test." So the Lithoprobe project tests the rocks of the Earth.

Lithoprobe began in 1984 as a small study at the University of British Columbia. When the last Dancing Elephant results were written up in 2003, the project had employed more than 900 scientists and cost upward of $100 million—or a little more than 2¢ for every year of the Earth's history. Federal and provincial governments, universities and private companies had all contributed to work in 10 study areas—

called transects (see map). The results changed many ideas regarding the geology of Canada and Lithoprobe was hailed worldwide as an unparalleled success.

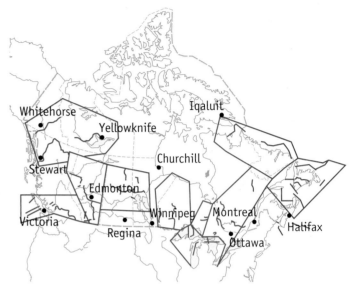

large, oddly shaped islands surrounded by a huge ocean dotted with smaller islands. Even a mere 70 million years ago, when the dinosaurs were walking around, you would have a hard time spotting anything familiar—still no Great Lakes,

a broad sea where Alberta, Saskatchewan and Manitoba are now, and hardly any Rocky Mountains.

Canada has changed throughout the Earth's history. Canada is still changing. And no map of the surface can show that. These changes can only be seen by looking where the Dancing Elephants look, at the dimensions of depth and time. Although we can't travel back in time, remnants of what happened in Canada millions of years ago are preserved deep below our feet. When we look down, we are also looking back.

This is what the Lithoprobe scientists have done. They have looked down and back to show us what is happening to Canada now, and what happened long ago. This may not seem much like the maps Cabot made so long ago, but Lithoprobe's work is just as important.

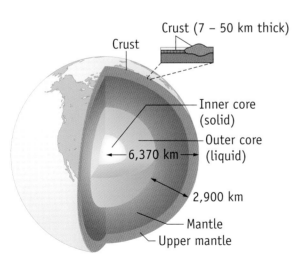

The earth beneath your feet is made up of many different layers.

10 Time and Time Again

Before we explore Lithoprobe's amazing discoveries, we need to spend a little time on time. What is time? It's how we measure what happens, from the few extra minutes of sleep we try to squeeze in each morning to the long-ago past in the stories our grandparents tell us. Time stretches back past Christopher Columbus, Julius Caesar and Homer to the dinosaurs, the first squiggles of life in the oceans, the birth of the world and other things that we can't even imagine.

In the pages that follow, you are going to read about events that happened so long ago that they are difficult to imagine. The timeline on the next page should help. Along both sides, it shows the different eras of the Earth's history and when the events described in this book happened. In the middle column, it shows you when these events might have happened if they took place over a school day instead of billions of years.

Still difficult to grasp, isn't it? Try this. Imagine that the world was formed at 9 a.m.—the beginning of your school day. Right now, as you sit here reading this book, it's 3 p.m. and the bell is sounding to send everyone home after a very busy day. A lot of that busyness—in fact, all of the time that's passed since your ancestors first became recognizably human—took place in the last 3 million years, or the final 14 seconds before the bell. Even that last second is 212,963 years!

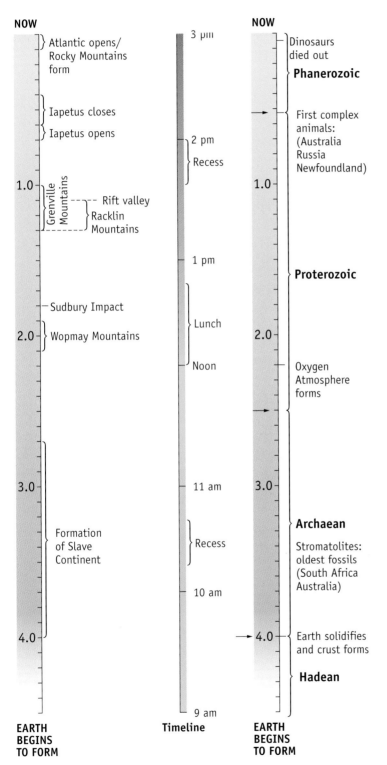

NOW

- ⟩ Atlantic opens/ Rocky Mountains form
- ⟩ Iapetus closes
- ⟩ Iapetus opens

1.0

Grenville Mountains
- − − Rift valley
- ⟩ Racklin Mountains

- − Sudbury Impact
- ⟩ Wopmay Mountains

2.0

3.0

Formation of Slave Continent

4.0

EARTH BEGINS TO FORM

Timeline

- 3 pm
- 2 pm
- ⟩ Recess
- 1 pm
- ⟩ Lunch
- Noon
- 11 am
- ⟩ Recess
- 10 am
- 9 am

NOW

- ⟩ Dinosaurs died out
- **Phanerozoic**
- ⟩ First complex animals: (Australia Russia Newfoundland)

1.0

- **Proterozoic**

2.0

- Oxygen Atmosphere forms

3.0

- **Archaean**
- Stromatolites: oldest fossils (South Africa Australia)

4.0
- ⟩ Earth solidifies and crust forms
- **Hadean**

EARTH BEGINS TO FORM

WHAT'S A MILLION?

A minute, an hour, a day, a week, a month, a year—those are understandable. But a million years? A billion?

Here's a million. Say the word "Mississippi." That should take you about a second (or 212,963 years). Say it again. Again. Again. Keep saying it. Don't eat. Don't go to the bathroom. Don't sleep. About eleven and a half days from now you will have said it a million times. In 31 years, you'll reach a billion. In about 143 years you will reach 4.6 billion. That's how old the Earth is: 4.6 billion years or 143 years worth of seconds.

So let's look at what Lithoprobe found out—in real time and in your school day— and let's do it backward, from the home bell (right now) to the opening bell (the formation of the Earth).

12 Getting Back on British Columbia

The west coast of Canada seems to have it made. While the rest of the country is still shoveling out from under winter's snowfall, west coasters are already admiring their daffodils. The British Columbia coast enjoys the mildest weather in Canada. Is it any wonder that some residents take great pleasure in gloating? If you don't happen to live there, never fear. There's a really easy way to get back at those people. Next time it's 15 below and snowing where you are and someone from Victoria asks what your weather is like, ask them if they noticed yesterday's earthquake.

Chances are the person on the other end of the phone will say, "No." That's your opportunity to add an interesting fact. "That's odd," you can say, "because there is an earthquake somewhere in British Columbia every day of every year."

If it's particularly cold where you are, you can mention that British Columbia shakes more than any other Canadian province. (There's no need to say that most of these rumblings are deep in the Earth and too weak to be felt.) If you're in a really mean mood, you can also tell them that some scientists are convinced that British Columbia is overdue for a mega-quake—the kind that can cause massive devastation and death.

The last big earthquake in British Columbia that most people felt happened

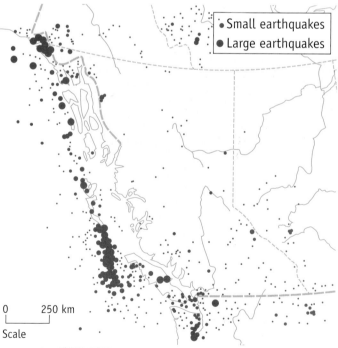

Scale 0 250 km

Earthquakes happen all over BC, but really big ones are concentrated offshore where the North American Plate meets the Pacific Plate.

RATING A QUAKE

The magnitude of an earthquake has usually been measured by the Richter scale. The Richter scale is determined by looking at the size of the squiggle an earthquake makes on a seismograph—a machine that records vibrations in the ground. It is an open-ended scale, but a small quake that few people even notice would be a 2 or 3, while a big one that destroys much of a city would be a 7 or 8.

In recent years, scientists have begun using the Moment Magnitude scale. This is similar to the Richter scale but more accurate and more complicated as it takes into account rock strength and the amount of movement along a fault.

Earthquakes, even small ones like the one near Plattsburgh in New York State in the upper picture, can cause a lot of damage. The lower picture shows the Courtenay school in 1946. Fortunately, it was a Sunday.

one Sunday morning in June 1946 near Courtenay on Vancouver Island (that's about 0.0003 of a second before the final bell!). On that Sunday, windows shattered, chimneys collapsed, kitchen crockery flew dangerously through the air and the main

street in the coal town of Cumberland rippled as if it was made of water. And this was a moderate earthquake! If the same quake were to happen today beneath Vancouver or Victoria, it would cause massive damage and loss of life. But big is relative. The Courtenay quake was nothing compared to what happened approximately 300 years ago.

"No One Survived"

January 26, 1700 (in the last second of your school day) was an ordinary day. As the evening wore on, some people in the First Nations' village at Pachina Bay on the west coast of Vancouver Island went to sleep. Others sat talking around the glowing embers of dying fires. Life was good. These people had lived in this area for generations and were experts at extracting the essentials of life from the forests, beaches and waters around them. They knew the cycles of the seasons and the ways of the animals. They knew the habits of the land and the sea. But nature had a brutal surprise in store for them that night.

The first violent movements shocked the sleepers awake, threw the talkers around and scattered the fires. As the Earth heaved and buckled, terrified families huddled together praying that the shaking would stop. Eventually it did, and the roaring of the Earth was replaced by the wails of the frightened and the cries of the injured. Stunned figures stumbled around in the dark.

Then the wave hit. A 10-meter-high wall of water roared up the beach with the speed of an express train. Trees, shelters, canoes and people were swept away. When the water receded, nothing was left of the Pachina Bay village or its inhabitants.

That terrible night is still vividly remembered by First Nations' elders: "... they simply had no time to get hold of canoes, no time to get awake. They

Earthquake devestation in Colombia, South America.

sank at once, were all drowned; no one survived."

Today, we know about this dreadful event because scientists can see its results in buried soils, drowned trees and seashells found in freshwater lakes far from the coast. We also know when it occurred—about 9 p.m. on that January night. Although this was almost a century before Europeans began keeping written records, the quake was strong enough to send waves completely across the Pacific Ocean where observers in Japan recorded their arrival. No earthquake was felt in

QUAKING IN YOUR BOOTS

Huge earthquakes are not unknown. Three very large ones were centered on New Madrid, Missouri, in 1811 and 1812. If they happened again today, thousands of people would be killed. More recently, huge quakes hit Alaska in 1964, Chile in 1960, the Aleutian Islands in 1957 and Kamchatka, Russia, in 1954. If any of them had occurred beneath a large city, the devastation and death would have been terrible. All were much larger than the Kobe, Japan, earthquake of 1995 that killed more than 5,000 people—and the earthquake that's coming off Canada's west coast could dwarf all of these tremblings.

Japan at the time, and scientists have concluded that the source originated from Canada's west coast.

Rock

Blocks

The Pachina Bay people were wiped out by a mega-quake, a very different thing from the one that frightened the residents of Courtenay about 250 years later, but the underlying causes were very similar.

The Courtenay earthquake happened because two blocks of rock on Vancouver Island were under extreme pressure—pressure strong enough to cause them to suddenly move. Take the tip of your finger and press it hard against this page. Keep pressing until your finger begins to move. Does your finger move smoothly? No. It moves up the page in little jerks, and the jerks get bigger the harder you press.

That is exactly what happened outside Courtenay. Two blocks of rock (picture your finger as one and this page as the other) were being pressed together. Like your finger on the page, the movement was jerky. That Sunday morning, Vancouver Island shook so much that people in Portland, Oregon, felt it.

Earthquakes are caused when two blocks of rock move against one another along a fault. This image shows how two blocks of rock moved to cause the Courtenay earthquake.

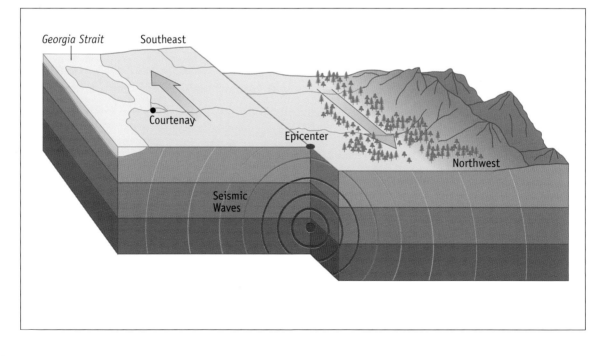

Georgia Strait   Southeast

Courtenay

Epicenter

Northwest

Seismic Waves

SUBDUCTION ZONES

The area where two plates of the Earth's crust meet and one is forced down beneath the other—like on Canada's west coast—is called a subduction zone. North America's west coast isn't the only subduction zone on the planet. Other ones like it exist off the west coast of South America, the north island of New Zealand and the Pacific side of Japan.

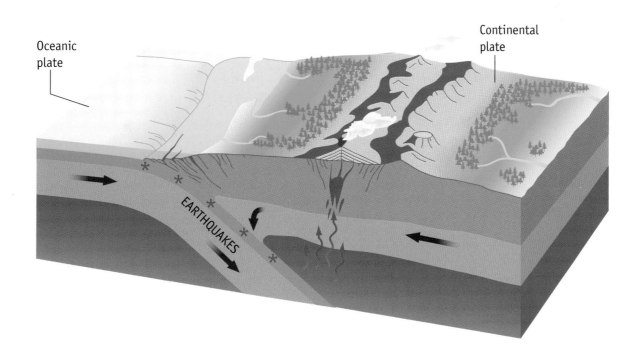

Oceanic plate

Continental plate

EARTHQUAKES

The Pachina Bay mega-quake was also caused by two blocks of rock moving against each other. The difference was that, in 1700, one of the blocks was Canada and the other was the bed of the Pacific Ocean. These continent-sized blocks needed much more energy to get them to move. When the jerk came, it was much stronger than the one at Courtenay.

But so what, you're probably saying, this all happened way in the past. And continents aren't moving around today, right? Wrong!

As the bell rings to end your school day, India is crashing into Asia with a force that makes the Titanic's encounter with an iceberg look like a fly bumping into a windowpane. And Canada is moving, too. Although it's happening very slowly (about the same rate as your fingernail grows), the distance from Toronto to Paris increases by about 4 centimeters every year. That means that the Atlantic Ocean is getting wider. And that means that the other side of Canada, the west coast, is slowly moving out into the Pacific Ocean.

So what does all of this mean? It means that the rock at the bottom of the Pacific Ocean is being pulverized by the country on which we live. Some of it is being scraped off and squashed up to form the thick sediments off British Columbia's coast. The rest is being pushed down—far beneath Victoria and Vancouver. But some parts of this melt rise upward and form volcanoes like Mount Garibaldi and Mount St. Helen's. We can climb the Coast Mountains and look westward at pieces of older Pacific Ocean floor and the islands that have

One of results of moving continents is beautiful scenery like this in the Coast Mountains of BC.

PLATE TECTONICS

Have you ever wondered why Africa and South America look as if they are separated pieces of a jigsaw puzzle? It's because they are! The Earth's crust is made up of seven large and

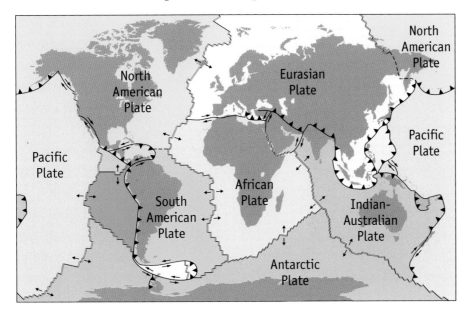

many smaller plates of rock that are continually moving around and bumping into each other. Some of the plates are broken bits of continents, like South America and Africa; others are hidden under the oceans. All are still moving—like pieces of a vast jigsaw puzzle that is continually breaking apart and reforming over millions of years. This process is called plate tectonics.

squished up, but the only way we can see the rocks that have been pushed down is by using Dancing Elephants.

The Dancing Elephants that worked on Canada's west coast did just that, and what they saw explained a lot about the province's frequent rumblings. Scientists now know that the floor of the Pacific Ocean is not being pushed smoothly beneath Canada. It jerks and shudders, just as your finger did moving up the page. These jerks and shudders act just like the Dancing Elephants' hammers: they send out shock waves, shock waves that we don't need microphones and computers to detect. We feel them as earthquakes. The bigger the jerks and shudders, the bigger the quake.

So far, British Columbia residents have been lucky—since the 1700s, quakes in the area have been small and relatively uneventful compared with the expected big one to come. But that could change at any time.

Eating Islands

The story of the next mega-quake that's likely to hit Canada's west coast began tens of millions of years ago. At that time (around 2:52 p.m.), there was an ocean off Canada's west coast, but not the one that is there today. This ancient ocean was dotted with large islands. Some were pieces of the continent that had broken off long before. Others were partly submerged mountain ranges made up of extinct volcanoes.

For the last 8 minutes of your school day, Canada has been moving west. It is being pushed from below by movement in the Earth's mantle—the area underneath the Earth's crust—and it is unstoppable.

While Canada has been moving west at a few centimeters a year, the dinosaurs have risen to dominate the land and then disappeared; birds have taken to the air; and insignificant rat-like animals have evolved into humans.

All during that time—over years, decades, centuries and millennia—Canada kept moving and growing. When there was nothing in the way, the land plowed through the crust beneath the ocean like an icebreaker through frozen Arctic waters. But not even huge islands could stop a continent on the move. One by one, they were either absorbed or destroyed. Sometimes, part of an island would be pushed under the continent, down into

Canada is moving west and scooping up old islands like Wrangellia, which now form most of Vancouver Island and extends under the lower mainland.

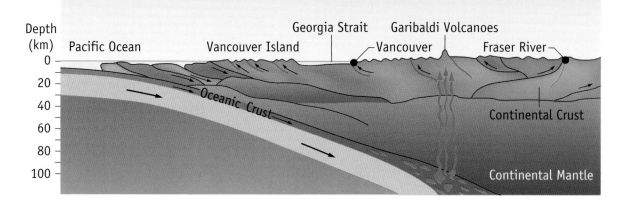

A GIANT'S JIGSAW

A geological map of British Columbia's west coast paints a very clear picture of how Canada has evolved. If you draw a line from Nelson to Watson Lake, and map a 500-kilometer-wide strip west of that line, the result looks like a giant's jigsaw puzzle. There are 21 pieces to the puzzle and it has taken 600 million years to put it together. Each piece has a name: Wrangellia, Stikinia, Quesnellia, Chilliwack-Nooksack, Monashee and Yakutat are just a few. They seem like magic names for long-vanished islands where unimaginable events took place, and in a way they are. But today, these places are all part of Canada.

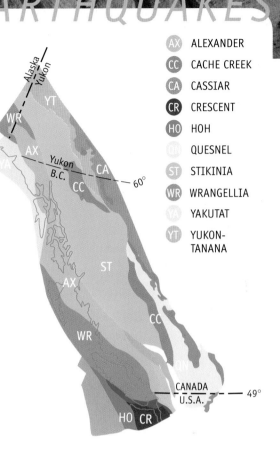

- (AX) ALEXANDER
- (CC) CACHE CREEK
- (CA) CASSIAR
- (CR) CRESCENT
- (HO) HOH
- (QN) QUESNEL
- (ST) STIKINIA
- (WR) WRANGELLIA
- (YA) YAKUTAT
- (YT) YUKON-TANANA

the immense heat and pressure of the mantle. It would melt there, and return to the surface as lava to feed the line of volcanoes stretching from California to British Columbia. Other times, part of an island would be pushed up and welded to the edge of the continent. It is a process that is still happening today and Lithoprobe lets us watch.

The Dancing Elephants, along with special ships that listen for the shock waves from explosions of compressed air set off at sea, have created a picture of Canada's west coast from out in the Pacific Ocean to the Rocky Mountains. This picture shows the floor of the ocean bending down, down, down—beneath Vancouver Island, the Strait of Georgia and the Coast Mountains. At a depth of around 100 kilometers, the ocean floor begins to melt and supply the heat and lava that fuels Mounts Baker, Garibaldi and St. Helens. The picture also shows the new bits of Canada piling up off Vancouver Island, and a piece of crust called Wrangellia (see sidebar) stretching from the surface of Vancouver Island to far beneath the mainland. To the east, other pieces of this ancient jigsaw are also visible. And, far below, we can see the mantle, the motor that is slowly but unstoppably dragging Canada toward the next chapter in its story.

On Shaky Ground

Will that chapter be a mega-quake? Many scientists believe that it will be. Why? At the moment, Canada is not sliding smoothly over the Pacific Ocean's floor. In fact, it is locked solid. Place your right hand out flat on the table in front of you, palm down. Lock your fingertips against the table and try to push your hand forward. As you push, the back of your hand bulges up.

That is exactly what is happening on Canada's west coast. As the continent struggles to continue moving westward— powered by immense forces within the mantle—the coastline is bulging up. In fact, Vancouver Island is rising about 4 millimeters every year, and Victoria is 7 millimeters closer to Penticton than it was a year ago.

Eventually, if you keep pushing your hand on the table, your fingers will slip forward and your palm will flatten against the tabletop. It's the same on Canada's west coast. Eventually, the forces will be too great and Canada will jerk west. Vancouver Island will drop a meter or two and Victoria will move away from Penticton. We will feel this jerk as a mega-quake—the most powerful kind of earthquake in the world.

Mega-quakes seem to happen off Canada's west coast about every 500 years. The last one wiped out the Pachina Bay people on that January night approximately 300 years ago. The next one might be 200 years away, or it might be tomorrow (just as the school bell finishes ringing). We'll just have to wait and see.

And where will the story end?

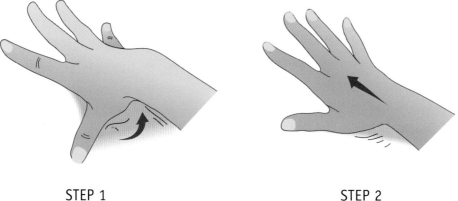

STEP 1   STEP 2

A view of the coast mountains from the city of Vancouver.

One day, millions of years in the future, Canada will stop moving westward. The mantle will run out of energy. Then there will be no more mega-quakes on the west coast. Perhaps Canada will even begin moving back in the other direction. Perhaps another ocean filled with huge islands will open up where the west coast is now. Perhaps the entire process will repeat itself. Who knows? Not even Lithoprobe can look that far into the future.

So British Columbia is the leading edge of Canada. Geologically, it's an exciting place to be (perhaps too exciting if you worry about earthquakes!). But the quaking coast is only part of Canada's story—and a very recent part at that. While British Columbia has been having all the fun, eating the floor of the Pacific Ocean, things have also been happening on the other side of the continent. We know that the world isn't getting any smaller, so if an old ocean is disappearing in one place, a young one must be forming somewhere else. It is, and Lithoprobe looked at that as well.

Walking on Africa

Giraffes strolling in their stately way across the Annapolis Valley; herds of zebra and wildebeest shuffling down dusty trails to drink at Shubenacadie Lake; lions bringing down terrified gazelle in a flurry of ripping claws and flying hooves in the middle of Halifax's main street.

Sound like a fantasy? It does, but when you stand in downtown Halifax, or Lunenburg or Yarmouth, there is actually more of Africa beneath your feet than Canada. In fact, almost all of Nova Scotia south of Truro is actually Africa—at least to a geologist.

Remember the giant's jigsaw puzzle of British Columbia? It showed us that continents can grow by scooping up pieces of whatever they bump into on their travels. But there's another side to the story. Huge scars in the Earth—scars that can only be seen clearly by looking deep below the surface—show us that continents can also break apart.

Take a piece of Plasticine (or firm play-dough) and mold it into a square about 5 centimeters on each side and about half a centimeter thick. Grip two opposite sides firmly and slowly pull your hands apart. First, the Plasticine will stretch, and then, thin cracks will begin to show on the surface. The more you pull, the more cracks will appear. Finally, some cracks will break

The piece of Africa that forms most of Nova Scotia is called Meguma by geologists.

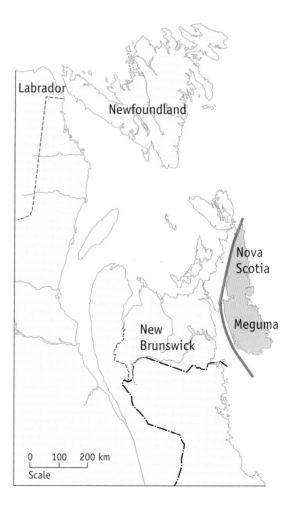

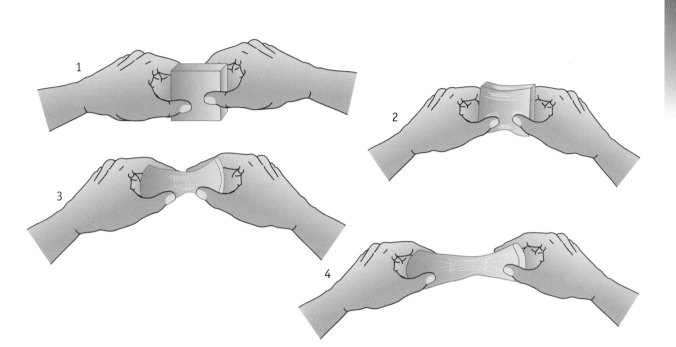

through the Plasticine. Pull long and hard enough, and you'll eventually have two pieces of Plasticine with only air in between.

Now, think of that piece of Plasticine as the Earth's crust and your hands as two incredibly strong forces ripping a continent apart. Say your left hand is pulling what will become North America and your right is pulling Africa and Europe. The Earth's crust would thin and crack just as the Plasticine did. And when the cracks eventually broke all the way through, hot lava would squish up from the mantle below to fill the hole. Water would also collect in the hollow on top of the thinned crust.

Presto! You've just made the Atlantic Ocean.

Cracking Up

East Africa rift valley.

Actually, in the real world, making an ocean the size of the Atlantic is not quite so simple. Sometimes the stretching works, and sometimes it doesn't.

In east Africa, there are a series of steep-walled valleys that really are filled with lions and zebra and wildebeest. They are called rift valleys, and they form when the Earth's crust cracks as it begins to pull apart. They are a much bigger version of the cracks you created in your Plasticine, and they are the first stage in the breaking up of a continent.

India used to be a part of Africa. Then it broke away, drifted north and crashed into Asia with such extraordinary force that it formed the Himalayan mountain range. Arabia was also once attached to Africa. When it broke away (25 million years ago or 2:58 p.m.), the Red Sea formed in its wake. East Africa's rift valleys might be the edges of the next pieces to break off.

Cracks in the Earth's crust—like the ones that help create rift valleys—are called faults, and when the rocks on either side of a fault move, you get an earthquake. When a continent is being pulled apart and two faults form side by side, the block of crust between them drops down. This sunken block forms a rift valley. This is exactly what has happened in east Africa. These valleys have not sunk deeply enough into the Earth's surface to allow lava from the mantle to push up into

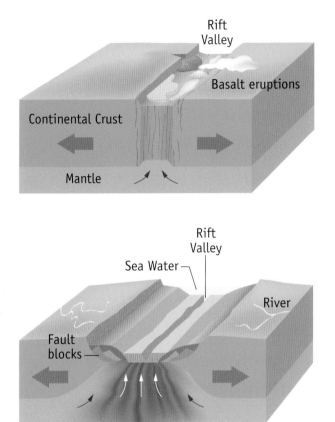

How rift valleys form.

them, or to let water flood over them, so there's no sea running down east Africa, but one day there might be. No one is certain whether the pulling apart of Africa is finished or just beginning, but we do know that it's not a new process, because Lithoprobe has seen where it happened long ago.

IS IT YOUR FAULT?

The cracks that form when a continent is put under pressure are called faults. There are many different kinds, depending on whether the blocks of rock are moving up, down or sideway. Some are deep in the Earth and can only be seen by Lithoprobe, while others are visible on the Earth's surface.

One of the Earth's most famous faults is California's San Andreas Fault. It is actually a complex system of faults that runs for more than 1,200 kilometers along the California coast. The western side of the fault—the Pacific Plate—is moving northwest relative to the eastern side—the North American Plate. Although it extends 16 kilometers into the Earth, the San Andreas Fault system can also be easily seen at the surface.

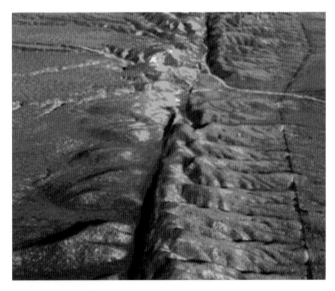

San Andreas Fault.

Six hundred million years ago—or about 2:12 p.m. in your school day—North America was part of a huge supercontinent called Laurentia. The east coast of Canada was attached to Greenland, Europe and the northern tip of Africa. Then the strain in the mantle began to build. First, rift valleys formed. But unlike in Africa, the process kept going. Eventually, North America split off from Europe and Africa, and between 600 million and 475 million years ago (2:12–2:23 p.m.) an ocean the size of the Atlantic formed. It was called Iapetus.

Then an odd thing happened. Instead of continuing to drag North America and Europe apart, or stopping and leaving them where they were, the forces in the mantle reversed. Very slowly, the two new continents came back together. This rejoining took 200 million years, and during the process, Canada's east coast would have looked much like the west coast does today: mountains formed, oceans shrank, a jigsaw puzzle of pieces was swept up as the continent grew and the ground shook with some pretty large earthquakes. Finally, 275 million years ago

The Appalachian Mountains once looked much more like the Rockies, but time has worn them down to these gentler, rolling hills.

(2:40 p.m.), the continents were back where they started.

Although it was a slow process, this meeting was so violent that it formed mountains still visible today. In North America they are called the Appalachians, and in the Highlands of Scotland and Scandinavia, they are called the Caledonides. They are old mountains, worn down and eroded by time and weather, and they are all that is left of the scar in the Earth that formed where Iapetus closed.

But even then, the mantle wasn't finished. The next chapter in the story began when the mysterious forces once more

reversed themselves and began pulling the continent apart. This time, new rift valleys cut across the land where Iapetus had been. When the continent broke apart again, a section was left in Europe (the Caledonides) and another part was carried off on the new continent of North America (the Appalachians).

About 100 million years ago (2:52 p.m.), when the dinosaurs were at their height, Canada split off from Spain and North Africa. Around 30 million years later (2:55 p.m.), when the age of dinosaurs was reaching its end, Canada left Northern Europe behind. Ever since, North America has been moving slowly but steadily west, and the Atlantic Ocean has been growing.

But because the Atlantic didn't form exactly where Iapetus had been, bits and pieces of the earlier continents became confused. A small piece of the old North America was left behind on the west coast of Scotland, a piece of Greenland was carried off with Canada and a chunk of Africa came traveling with us to form most of Nova Scotia.

But even before Iapetus, Canada nearly broke apart.

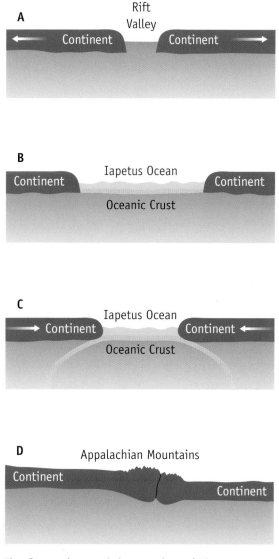

The formation and destruction of the Iapetus Ocean.

Today it takes two or three days to drive from Winnipeg to Chicago. Good roads lead you past some pretty scenery, and lots of small towns full of places to eat and sleep. The trip would make a nice family holiday. However, 1.1 billion years ago (1:35 p.m.), it would have been a very different story.

algae, but that's it. What life there is remains confined to the ocean.

Around halfway to Chicago, you come to the most exciting portion of your journey. As you approach what is now Duluth, you begin to wind down into a deep valley. Since it's a long way down, and since there's no vegetation to stabilize the hillsides, it's a thrilling ride. And the valley floor is no easier. For 50 kilometers or so, the ground is fairly flat, but it's not quiet. Recent lava flows are all around,

Leaving Winnipeg, you travel over barren landscape, probably similar to the surface of the moon. There are no trees, bushes, grass or vegetation. You don't worry about animals running out onto the road, because there are none. The odd stagnant pool of water might contain some

some still hissing into the large lakes on either side of you. The ground is hot, and yellow sulphurous smoke rises out of cracks in the Earth and from the summits of small volcanoes. It's so unpleasant that you're glad when you begin the long hard haul up the other side of the valley.

A CLOSE CALL

Even before Lithoprobe, scientists knew that there was a rift valley beneath Lake Superior. What surprised them when the squiggly lines came out of the computer was how big it was. Lithoprobe's findings showed that the crust beneath the rift was much thinner than expected, which meant that North America had come closer to splitting apart than previously thought.

If you'd actually taken that drive, you would probably have felt like you were inside the crater of an active volcano—and you would have been. It was a crater that ran for 2,000 kilometers from Kansas to Michigan; a crater that Lithoprobe looked at where it is buried deep beneath Lake Superior; a crater that almost ripped North America apart.

Beneath you on that imaginary drive, the vast forces that drag continents around the surface of the Earth were pulling in opposite directions. The stress was tearing the land apart and creating rift valleys. But the process you witnessed was going further. The valley you crossed kept sinking. Seawater poured in and the valley eventually filled with alternating layers of lava from beneath and sediment washing down from the valley sides above. Lithoprobe spotted these layers. There are 30 kilometers of them in total—15 times the depth of the Grand Canyon. If the forces had kept going, there would have been an ocean for you to cross on your holiday. Imagine the Atlantic between Chicago and Winnipeg.

But the process didn't continue. Everything stopped. The huge volcanoes that fed lava onto the valley floor petered out. The seawater retreated. Everything settled down and the rift valley was buried to await Lithoprobe's inquiring eye.

But the forces within the Earth never stop working. Things are always changing. Oceans open and close, continents break apart and reform—and mountains rise and fall.

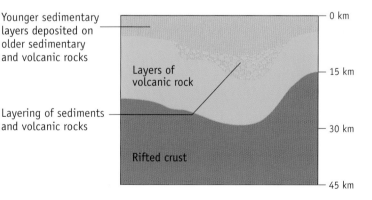

Younger sedimentary layers deposited on older sedimentary and volcanic rocks

Layers of volcanic rock

Layering of sediments and volcanic rocks

Rifted crust

0 km

15 km

30 km

45 km

The Dancing Elephants showed the shape of the buried rift valley below Lake Superior.

Mountains You Can't See

How about this for a weekend excursion from Toronto? Get your parents to drive a couple of hours north into the Grenville Mountains. If it's winter, take a ski lift at one of the many resorts, or snowshoe across the back country. If it's summer, hike up through the trees into the alpine meadows and enjoy the panoramic views. You might also do some rock climbing or whitewater rafting. The possibilities are endless.

Whatever you do, you will be surrounded by interesting people. Most have come, like you, to enjoy the varied activities. Some, however, are serious mountain climbers. You can identify them by their weather-beaten faces and the intense way they go about things. Perhaps they have just come down from the summit of Mount Grenville, the highest mountain on Earth. You look at them with awe. They have been up in the death zone where the air is so thin it is

Perhaps mountaineering in the mighty Grenville Mountains might have looked like this.

Mount Everest, Himalaya Mountains.

UPS AND DOWNS

At 8,848 meters above sea level, Mount Everest is the highest point on the surface of the Earth. It and the next 13 highest mountains in the world are in the Himalayas. They are so high that there is always a gale blowing up there and there is so little oxygen that you can barely breathe. Every step takes an immense effort. The very tops of the world's highest mountains are called "death zones" because a lot of climbers never make it down. More than 140 have died on Everest alone.

almost impossible to drag enough oxygen into tortured lungs, and where the violent wind and biting cold are so brutal and harsh that few people ever go there—and even fewer return alive.

But wait a minute! There are no mountains north of Toronto. You know this because mountains are easy to recognize. They stick up into the air, are often covered with snow and are good places to build ski resorts. But what if mountains didn't stick up? What if you didn't need fancy climbing gear and oxygen to climb them? What if you could walk over them without noticing? How would you know they were mountains at all? You wouldn't—not without Lithoprobe and the Dancing Elephants.

India in Your Bathtub

One of the neat things about mountains is that they go down as well as up. Mountains are not just lumps of the Earth's crust sitting on top of the mantle, they sink down into it, too. So, the Himalayas are both the highest and lowest mountains on Earth today.

Try this experiment. Take a block of wood and float it in a bathtub full of water. Some of the block sticks up above the water's surface and some sinks below. Now, take a larger block of wood and put it beside the first one. It stands up higher than the smaller block, but it also sinks down farther. Try pieces of wood in different shapes and sizes (rectangular is best, but cubes work well too because they tend to tilt onto their edges and look more like mountains). The larger the block, the more it will sink into the water.

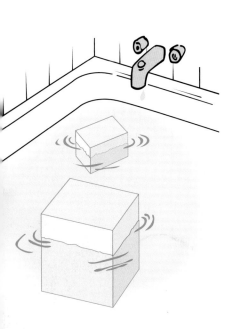

A few pages back, you made the Atlantic Ocean with Plasticine; now you've made the Himalayas. The water in your tub is the Earth's mantle and the blocks of wood are the crust. The crust floats on the mantle in the same way as the blocks float on water. The thicker the crust, the higher it will stand—and the lower it will sink. The crust that makes up the Himalayas is the thickest on the planet.

After India broke away from Africa around 200 million years ago (2:45 p.m.), it drifted north until it collided with Asia. Slowly, the edges of these two continents crumbled and buckled. There must have been some big earthquakes when that happened, but fortunately, there were no people around to feel them.

Gradually, India was pushed under Asia and, about 50 million years ago (2:56 p.m.), the Himalayas began forming. Take two blocks of wood and place one on top of the other (you might need to stick them together with a blob of Plasticine). Now see how they float. The top will be higher than if you had used a single block, and the bottom will sink deeper into the water. The high bit is Mount Everest and the low bit is what is going on below the ground. The Himalayas are the highest mountains in the world because the crust there is twice as thick in comparison to other places.

The bit of the Himalayas that pushes down into the mantle is known as the root

Himalyas

India   Asia

The Earth's crust is twice its usual thickness where India is pushed beneath Asia.

of the mountains. All mountain ranges have roots and people have known about them for more than 100 years. So what do mountain roots on the other side of the world have to do with Canada? You guessed it— Lithoprobe's pictures of the Grenville Mountains.

DISCOVERING ROOTS

In the 19th century, surveyors in India noticed that their instruments were behaving oddly. When you stand by the Ganges River in north India and hang a lead weight on a string, it will be attracted very slightly toward the Himalaya Mountains. This is perfectly normal because large dense masses attract things to them. The force is called gravity and you know about it because planets attract things in space. But smaller things than planets exert the pull of gravity, it's just much

weaker. The odd thing about the lead weights in India was that they were not pulled as strongly toward the Himalayas as they should have been. Either the mountains were hollow, which seemed unlikely, or there was a large unseen mass of less dense mountain rock (the Earth's crust) below the Himalayas where dense mantle rock should have been. That was how people discovered that mountains have roots—they just weren't able to see them until Lithoprobe came along.

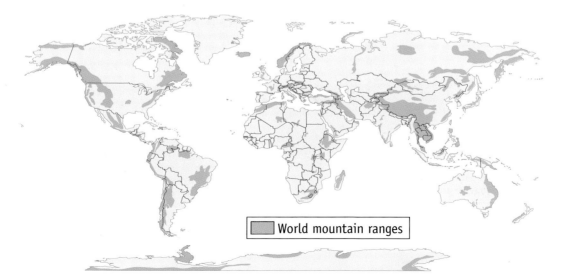

World mountain ranges

Make Your Own Mountains

Canada is quite well off as far as mountains go. Today, we have the Rocky, the Coast and Mackenzie Mountains, and the Appalachians. But we used to have more.

Between 1.3 billion and 1 billion years ago (1:20–1:45 p.m.), one of the greatest events in the Earth's history took place. Two massive continents met to form one supercontinent called Rodinia. The line where they joined runs for 5,000 kilometers from Mexico to Labrador, and even

across the Atlantic into Sweden. Part of this line was the Grenville Mountains.

This was a collision of awesome proportions. The pieces of continent scooped up more recently by Canada's west coast are mere bumps compared to it. Even India crashing into Asia cannot compare.

Take a baking tray and cover it with a thin layer of cooking oil. Now take the two pieces of Plasticine you created when you formed the Atlantic Ocean and move them around until they slide easily on the tray. Slowly bring them together. See how the edges crumple as you push harder? See how the edges mound up as you keep on pushing? The more you push, the higher the ridge. If ants lived on one of your pieces of Plasticine, they would see mountains rising in front of them.

Imagine the world's continents and subcontinents in your two pieces of

Rock formations on the shore of Georgian Bay, Ontario—all that is left of the once towering Grenville Mountains.

Plasticine—Asia, North America and Europe in one, and Africa, India, South America, Antarctica and Australia in the other. Imagine that you are the ant and the few seconds it took to push the Plasticine together were actually millions of years. You would have witnessed the creation of the largest mountain range ever to exist on the planet. It was higher, wider and longer than the Himalayas. It was the Grenville Mountains.

If you want to climb the Grenville Mountains today, all you need to do is stroll up the gently sloping shore from Georgian Bay. You don't need base camps, special equipment or oxygen tanks. The highest mountains in the world are gone—worn down grain of sand by grain of sand

into oceans that themselves dried up millions of years before you were born.

But the bit below the ground is still there. Part of the Grenville Mountains' roots—once buried so deeply that it was almost melted by the mantle's heat and pressure—are exposed in the bare rocks you can stroll over beside Lake Huron. The Grenville Mountain's roots are only a scar now, and only Lithoprobe with its Dancing Elephants and special ships can see it properly. But it is a scar that was once magnificent; a scar that held together a supercontinent, at least until the forces that pushed the two pieces together changed direction and ripped them apart although not along the same scars.

Canada is old and it's picked up some pretty impressive scars through the ages. But not all of them are the result of continents moving.

So far, Lithoprobe has helped us imagine a weekend in the Grenville Mountains and a drive across the rift valley beneath Lake Superior. Perhaps there is another holiday you would like to take—to southern Alberta 65 million years ago (2:55 p.m.). Once you arrived, you could stroll through the cypress trees by the shores of the Bearpaw Sea while pterosaurs soared above, plesiosaurs frolicked in the surf and herds of duck-billed dinosaurs lumbered past. But the holiday might not have the ending you would like.

Something—perhaps a strange agitation in the animals around you, perhaps a eerie light in the sky—makes you look up. What you see almost makes your heart stop. There are two suns in the sky. One is the right color and is where it should be; the other is an angry red and is streaking silently south. As the second sun vanishes over the horizon, the shriek of its journey reaches you. Then there is the flash of its impact, the thunder of an earthquake worse than any you can imagine and the howling winds of the blast wave. The sky rains fire and the world descends into a blackness that will last for months. If you survived—and 75 percent of life on Earth, including all the dinosaurs, did not—the planet would not be a pleasant place for a long time.

That second sun was really a meteor—10 kilometers wide and traveling at a speed of tens of kilometers a second. When it hit, the impact dug a hole 200 kilometers wide and deep enough to break through the Earth's crust where Mexico's Yucatán Peninsula is now.

A tyrannosaur watches the end of its world.

Barringer Meteorite Crater, Arizona.

Extraterrestrial visitors like this come to Earth regularly. Ones the size of peas arrive at a rate of about 10 every hour. Once a month a basketball-sized one touches down. Fortunately, millions of years pass between meteors the size of the one that killed the dinosaurs. But many past visitors have left scars.

In the Arizona desert, there is a hole in the ground 200 meters deep, over a kilometer wide and surrounded by blocks of rock the size of small houses. It is called the Barringer Crater, and it was made only 50,000 years ago (in the last second of your school day) by a visitor from space measuring a mere 50 meters across and weighing a paltry 300,000 tons.

Because of water and wind, the surface of the Earth is continually changing. Only very recent meteorite craters, like the one

SHOULD YOU BE NERVOUS?

What are your chances of being hit by a meteorite? Pretty slim really. There is no record of a human ever being killed by a meteorite, although in recent years small ones have crashed into a dining room in Connecticut, a bedroom in Alabama and a car in New York. The chances that in the next hundred years a really big one will cause as much damage as the one that killed the dinosaurs is about 1 in 500,000. So don't lose any sleep.

The scars left by meteorite impact—called astroblemes—can be found all over the world and they range in size from a few meters to hundreds of kilometers across. There are not as many as on the moon because erosion by rain and wind has destroyed many old ones or rivers and seas have covered them up with sediments. Canada is a good place to look for meteorites because much of its rock is very old.

in Arizona, are well preserved. But all the big ones leave scars and since much of Canada is very old, it is a good place to look for these scars.

and Mining

Canada's most famous meteorite scar was formed around 1.85 billion years ago (12:35 p.m.), long before Rodinia was tied together by the mighty Grenville Mountains. A 2-kilometer-wide piece of rock, traveling at 50,000 kilometers an hour (that's almost 14 kilometers every second!) plowed into what is now Ontario, digging a crater 70 kilometers across. Nickel and copper ore deep within the Earth's crust were melted and washed up to the surface. In examining the area, Lithoprobe discovered that the originally circular scar was pushed into an oval shape by underground forces and gradually eroded. Eventually, the town of Sudbury grew up on the site.

Some of the richest nickel and copper deposits in the world can be found around the Sudbury crater. The Dancing Elephants went there and helped geologists understand how these valuable metal deposits formed.

The moment of impact of the Sudbury meteorite.

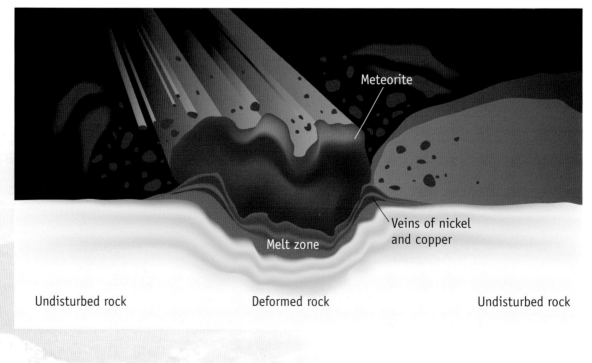

Undisturbed rock   Deformed rock   Undisturbed rock

Meteorite

Melt zone

Veins of nickel and copper

PENNIES FROM HEAVEN

Ten percent of all the nickel used in the world, including some that goes into your pennies, comes from mines in Sudbury. So does a lot of copper, gold and platinum—$3 billion a year's worth in fact. All this wealth was discovered in 1883 by Canadian Pacific Railway workers who, as a hobby in their spare time, went prospecting for minerals in the new cuts for the railbed. At first, the ore was dug out from the surface of the ground, but as demand increased and with the event of the First World War, mines were pushed ever deeper into the ground. Today, the Creighton nickel and copper mine in Sudbury is the deepest mine in Canada. Standing at its bottom, you have 2.2 kilometers of rock above your head.

Loading nickel ore in Sudbury, Ontario.

There are diamonds in the Northwest Territories—the Dancing Elephants were there. There is oil and gas in Alberta—the Dancing Elephants were there, too. They looked far down to the ancient rocks below to see if the story of continents colliding and separating could have had anything to do with these deposits. It is important to know where these vanished continents met and fell apart, not just for the story itself, but because it is at these places that minerals worth millions of dollars tend to collect.

Traditionally, prospectors looking for minerals have been hardy, rather eccentric people, struggling through swamps, wading up streams and swatting countless mosquitoes in a determined effort to strike it rich. Today, they are just as likely to be found poring over the maps and pictures that the Dancing Elephants helped to produce. They may not care about continents colliding and separating, or about mountains that were old before the dinosaurs walked, but perhaps they should. It's all part of the same story and there is only one bit left to tell.

The Oldest Piece of the Puzzle

So North America, and every other continent on the surface of the globe, is a patchwork of older pieces of continent crisscrossed by the scars of long-vanished mountain ranges. Supercontinents have formed and broken up over and over again. How many times and for how long?

No one knows the answer to the first part of that question. Some scientists believe that there is a cycle of continent formation and breakup. They suggest that every 500 million years or so (about every 40 minutes during your school day) the continents come together to form a single supercontinent. That supercontinent is so huge that heat from the mantle cannot escape and builds up underneath. Eventually enough heat builds to power the forces that split continents apart. Rift valleys and ocean basins form as the

How the continents have moved in the last 200 million years.

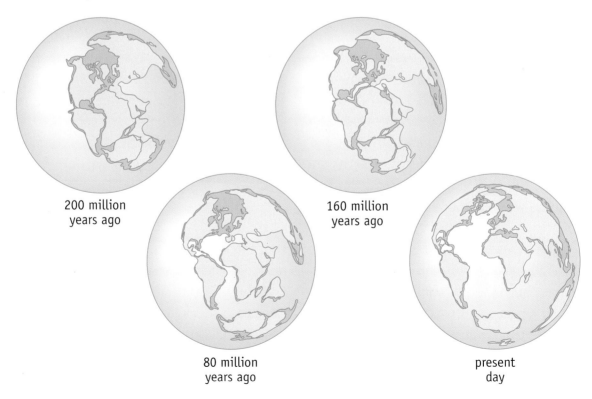

200 million
years ago

160 million
years ago

80 million
years ago

present
day

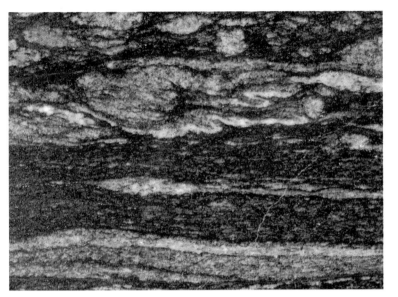

A polished slab of Acasta gneiss rock from the Slave Craton. This rock formed 3.96 billion years ago, around 9:45 in your school day.

of cosmic dust and debris circling the sun (around 9:45 a.m.). Today, a piece of that ancient rock—the oldest rock in the world—can still be seen in northern Canada's Slave Craton.

A visit to the Slave Continent would have been a nightmarish experience. For a start, you could not have breathed the thin atmosphere of toxic gases expelled from the huge volcanic eruptions all around. Meteors would streak through the thin atmosphere and crash to the ground leaving craters of all sizes. In the daytime you would bake; at night you would freeze. You would want to go home. But you would have to wait almost 4 billion years for home to exist.

supercontinent breaks up and its pieces drift farther away from each other. As they do, the heat escapes. Eventually, the continents stop moving and gradually begin coming back together until, 500 million years later, they form another supercontinent and the process is repeated.

Scientists know a bit about what may have been the first continent ever to form. It's called the Slave Continent, and it began forming only a few hundred million years after the Earth solidified from a band

The Same Old Story

The Slave Craton is the core of Canada—the first bit of continental crust around which other pieces gathered as North America wandered around the surface of the Earth. To the west of the Slave Craton, the growth of North America is recorded in strips of rock right out to the coast. Four billion years of the Earth's history in one place! It was an opportunity Lithoprobe could not resist.

What's left of the Slave Continent is different from later continents, but whether this is because it is a small, unusual piece or because all continents were different in those days, no one knows.

Geologists divide the ancient rocks of North America into Provinces, the remains of long-vanished continents and mountain ranges.

Certainly what happened after the Slave Continent formed is a familiar story.

To the west of the Slave Continent was an ocean dotted with volcanoes and pieces of the Earth's crust. Gradually, between 2.1 billion and 1.9 billion years ago (around 12:25 p.m.), these volcanoes and islands joined the edge of the Slave Continent to create a jigsaw puzzle of pieces and the Wopmay mountain range.

Sound familiar? Then an ocean formed and the process began all over again as new pieces were added to the jigsaw puzzle between 1.3 and 1.1 billion years ago

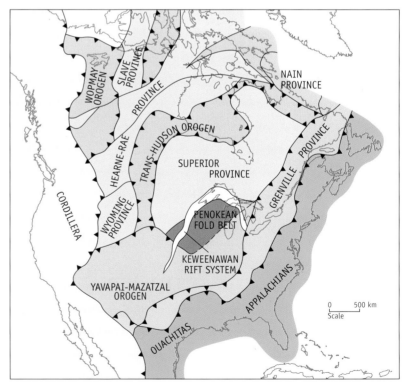

LITHOPROBE
AROUND THE WORLD

The results of Lithoprobe's research have been presented to thousands of scientists around the world and many similar projects are now being undertaken or proposed. In the United States, Earthscope is being set up to study the evolution of the entire continent. Part of this project is US Array, a Lithoprobe-like undertaking that aims to make a picture of the roots of the whole country. Some of the sites that will collect the information have already been built. In Europe, Europrobe has been partly inspired by Lithoprobe and, so far, has carried out 10 projects in 30 countries.

(around 1:30 p.m.)—just about the time the Grenville Mountains were forming. The Slave Continent was bigger by this time and the Wopmay Mountains had been worn down. The new pieces of the jigsaw were the Racklan Mountains.

Guess what happened next?

Right—an ocean formed. Then? Right again. The jigsaw began growing once more, bringing us back to the beginning— with earthquakes in British Columbia and Lithoprobe's work along Canada's west coast.

The whole of Canada, in fact the whole of North America, is a jigsaw puzzle of pieces of crust stuck together by what is left of ancient mountain ranges. Since the Slave Continent formed, when the Earth was very young, continents have come together to create mountains and broken apart to form oceans—and all the while, they've scooped up islands on their travels.

With the help of geologists and other scientists, we can see these things happening, both in Canada and on the other side of the world. Thanks to Lithoprobe's Dancing Elephants, we can also see that the same things happened long ago to the rocks far beneath your feet. Taken together, these two perspectives show us 4 billion years of history. It's quite a story; a story that will continue to play out for millions of years to come.

There are many good geology resources on the web, just do a search for the topic that interests you (for example: earthquakes, volcanic eruptions, etc.). Here are some of the best ones:

www.geop.ubc.ca/Lithoprobe
This is the Lithoprobe home page for all the latest stuff on the story beneath your feet. It is a bit technical, but there are some interesting places, such as the slides at
(www.science.ubc.ca/~eoswr/lithoprobe/slide.html)

www.earthscope.org/
This is the home page for the US Lithoprobe-like study.

www.geofys.uu.se/eprobe/
This is the home page for the European study.

www.nrcan.gc.ca/gsc/index_e.html
The Geological Survey of Canada home page. This site contains many cool links including:

Ask a Geologist
www.nrcan.gc.ca/ess/esic/cgi-bin/askageol_e.cgi
Earthquakes
www.seismo.nrcan.gc.ca/eqinfo/index_e.php
Meteorites
www.unb.ca/passc/ImpactDatabase/

Plate Tectonics
www.uky.edu/ArtsSciences/Geology/webdogs/plates/reconstructions.html

www.usgs.gov/
The US Geological Survey includes weekly reports on
earthquakes (earthquake.usgs.gov/) and volcanoes (volcanoes.usgs.gov/)

www.seismo.unr.edu/ftp/pub/louie/class/100/plate-tectonics.html
A site about plate tectonics.

www.ucmp.berkeley.edu/geology/tectonics.html
More plate tectonics but animated this time.

www.scotese.com
An excellent site with some really cool graphics and animations.

www.pbs.org/wgbh/aso/tryit/tectonics
This site includes some neat geology related activities.

www.geology.about.com/ and www.geologylink.com
These are two general sites that have some good activities and will link you to anywhere you want to go in the story of the earth.